Eco-Journey

EXPLORING
DESERTS

Eco-Journey

EXPLORING
DESERTS

Barbara J. Behm
Veronica Bonar

Gareth Stevens Publishing
MILWAUKEE

For a free color catalog describing Gareth Stevens' list of high-quality books, call 1-800-341-3569 (USA) or 1-800-461-9120 (Canada).

ISBN 0-8368-1063-5

North American edition first published in 1994 by
Gareth Stevens Publishing
1555 North RiverCenter Drive, Suite 201
Milwaukee, WI 53212, USA

Photographic acknowledgments
The publishers wish to acknowledge, with thanks, the following photographic sources:
t = top *b* = bottom
Cover: J. Allan Cash Photo Library; Title page: J. & D. Bartlett/Bruce Coleman Ltd.; pp. 6 Anthony Bannister/NHPA; 7 Jan Griffiths/Robert Harding Picture Library; 8 Anthony Bannister/ NHPA; 9*t* Gerald Cubitt/Bruce Coleman Ltd.; 9*b* John Shaw/NHPA; 10*t* John Visser/Bruce Coleman Ltd.; 10*b* Gerald Cubitt/Bruce Coleman Ltd., 11 M. Fogden/Bruce Coleman Ltd.; 12 Nigel Dennis/NHPA; 13*t*, 13*b* Anthony Bannister/NHPA; 14*t* Ashod Papazian/NHPA; 14*b* Michael Leech/NHPA; 15 Leonard Lee Rue/Bruce Coleman Ltd.; 16*t* Anthony Bannister/NHPA; 16*b* Wilkins/Bruce Coleman Ltd.; 17 G. Ziesler/Bruce Coleman Ltd.; 18*t* Rod Williams/Bruce Coleman Ltd., 18*b* Peter Johnson/NHPA; 19 Gerald Lacz/NHPA; 20, 21*t*, 21*b*, 22, 23*t* Anthony Bannister/NHPA; 23*b*, 24 Jane Burton/Bruce Coleman Ltd.; 25*t* Anthony Bannister/NHPA; 25*b* Norman Myers/Bruce Coleman Ltd.; 26 Peter Ward/Bruce Coleman Ltd.; 27*t* J. Meech/NHPA; 27*b* Nigel Dennis/NHPA.

Printed in the United States of America

1 2 3 4 5 6 7 8 9 99 98 97 96 95 94

Title page:
An ostrich can run nearly 40 miles
(65 kilometers) per hour.

CONTENTS

Words that appear in the glossary are printed in **boldface** type the first time they occur in the text.

This is the desert

Very little rain falls in the desert. The sun and the wind dry up any water or early morning dew.

▼ The wind has blown the sand into dunes, or hills.

Some areas of the desert have water at or near the surface of the land. These green areas of the desert are called **oases**.

▲ Desert soil is too dry for many types of plants to grow. At an oasis, however, palm trees and other plants are able to grow.

7

Desert plants

Desert plants often store water in their stems or roots. The leaves of some desert plants have a waxy coating to keep water in.

▶ Naras plants grow on the sandy desert floor. These plants have sharp thorns and tiny leaves. Their long roots find water deep in the ground. Some desert animals feed on the fruit.

◄ Acacia trees have small leaves and long roots that grow nearly 100 feet (30 meters) into the soil to find water. This acacia tree provides shelter for the termite nest beside it. The nest may have more than one million termites inside it.

▼ Euphorbia trees have prickly spines instead of leaves. Their stems store water in the form of a juice. Animals do not like the taste of this juice and will not eat the trees.

Some desert plants have wide, shallow roots. The roots spread out to take in dew and rainfall. Other plants have long roots that reach underground water.

9

The flowering desert

Sudden thunderstorms or a heavy shower of rain will bring the desert to life. Dry, yellowing plants turn green and flower.

▲ Some euphorbias are small, low-growing shrubs. They look like cactus plants. Flowers grow at the tips of their spiny stems.

▶ A sudden rain has left pools of water on the desert floor. The shrubs and plants burst into life.

◀ Desert flowers bloom only a very short time. Butterflies, moths, wasps, and bees **pollinate** the flowers. These insects, together with their eggs, provide food for spiders, scorpions, and many birds and reptiles that live in the desert.

Most desert plants live ten or fifteen days before the moisture disappears. They live just long enough to flower and produce seeds. The seeds may have to wait a year or more before it rains again to grow.

The search for water

Desert animals spend a lot of time looking for water. Large animals may travel a long way to find water.

▼ An oryx drinks at a desert watering hole.

◄ When the male sand grouse finds water, he first drinks for himself. Then he soaks his belly feathers in the water. The feathers absorb water like a sponge. Then he flies back to the nest. The chicks crowd around him and suck the water from his feathers.

▼ Desert ants drink from a droplet of water. Scientists think that the fine white hairs on the ants' backs help keep the ants cool.

A few animals never drink regular water at all. Some small animals get moisture from seeds. Antelopes get liquid from the juice in the leaves of plants. Foxes get liquid from the plants and animals they eat.

▲ The long-eared desert hedgehog lives in burrows during the day to keep cool. It comes out at night to feed on insects.

Saving water

Many desert insects and other small animals dig into the sand to escape the heat. They do not sweat in the cool underground **burrows**, and so their bodies lose less water.

▶ Prickly pears store water in their stems. The stems have a waterproof, waxy coating to prevent evaporation.

Camels have a thick, woolly hide that **insulates**, or protects, them from the hot sun. Their thick fur also slows evaporation when they sweat.

▲ A camel can go for up to ten days without drinking or eating. It lives on the fat that it stores in its hump.

Daytime in the desert

Many desert spiders and beetles eat during the day. Their hard, outer skin stops them from losing water by evaporation. Lizards run across the burning sand, hunting these animals.

▲ Oryx graze at night when the plants have dew on them.

▶ Dung beetles eat and gather animal droppings. They roll the dung into a ball.   The females lay eggs in the dung.

16

◄ Many owls hunt at night and spend the day resting in trees or cracks in rocks. The owls eat insects, reptiles, other birds, and even small deer. The color of an eagle owl's feathers **camouflages** it well in the desert.

Most desert birds hunt for insects and other food during the day. They rest during the midday heat.

Keeping cool

To keep cool in the desert, larger animals find shelter in the shade of a rock or a tree. Lizards find shelter in holes or under rocks. A squirrel shields itself with its tail when it comes out of its burrow.

▲ Dabb lizards burrow into the sand during the hottest part of the day.

▶ Springboks take shelter in the shade of an acacia tree. Acacias stay green all year through.

18

Panting draws air into the moist lining of an animal's mouth. The saliva in its mouth evaporates, and this cools the animal.

▲ The huge ears of a fennec fox cool its body. The blood vessels in the ears are very close to the surface. Air blowing across the ears cools the blood flowing through the vessels.

19

Moving over the desert

The feet of many desert animals have grown in special shapes, or **adapted**, to survive the desert.

▼ A sidewinder viper moves across the sand by rolling its body sideways in a series of S-loops. It makes tracks in the sand as it moves.

◄ A chameleon runs carefully on tiptoe across a desert road. The grasshopper on its back is getting a free ride! As the chameleon runs, it holds its body well away from the hot road surface. Its long tail helps it keep balanced.

▼ The long, thin legs of the wandering spider help it move easily over loose sand. Desert spiders hunt at night or dusk to avoid the heat of the day.

Camels have spread toes that keep them from sinking in the sand. Some lizards, such as geckoes, have webbed feet to keep them from sinking in the sand. Sand lizards push aside hot surface sand to walk on cool sand below.

Under the desert floor

Many desert animals live under the sand or in burrows to keep out of the sun. Fennec foxes dig a deep burrow.

▶ The hairlike fringes around a gecko's feet evenly spread the animal's weight. It can then skim over the desert easily, without disturbing the sand.

◄ Wolf spiders live in holes in the ground that they close with a trapdoor.

The desert viper buries itself in loose sand to cool down. Only its eyes show as it lies in wait for birds and rodents. Rodents called jerboas seal off their tunnels with sand to keep the hot air out.

▼ Mole rats live most of their lives in long tunnels in the ground. They live on water that is stored in roots of plants.

Desert nightlife

▶ When gerbils leave their burrows, they look around for danger. If they sense danger, they beat on the ground with their hind legs or cry out before returning to the burrow.

When night falls in the desert, the temperature drops very quickly. Heavy dew makes the ground damp.

Scorpions, spiders, centipedes, geckoes, and rodents all come out to hunt for insects. Gerbils and jerboas must watch for **predators**, such as foxes.

▲ A dune spider leaves the shelter of its burrow to hunt for insects. Desert spiders have a thin layer of wax on their bodies. The wax prevents them from losing water through evaporation.

◄ This scorpion has caught a caterpillar. Desert scorpions come out only at night. They do not see well and hunt by scent and touch.

Food in the desert

Plants are an important source of food for many animals. The gazelle and oryx eat only plants. They are called **herbivores**. In order to survive, plants must produce a large amount of seeds.

▶ This robber-fly has caught a butterfly. Robber-flies hunt every kind of flying insect.

◄ Desert lizards run quickly over the sand. They stand with their heads held high and their bodies clear of the hot sand.

▼ Falcons catch prey with their claws. After eating, they soar in the cool air above the desert.

Some desert animals can live without food for many days. Darkling beetles can survive for more than 130 days without eating. Desert animals, like desert plants, have to be tough in order to survive.

More Books To Read

Chase through the Desert Wilds. Christopher Carrie
   (Binney and Smith)

The Desert: A Nature Panorama. Susan Daming.

Desert Discovery: An Activity Book for Kids.
   (Double B Publications)

Deserts. Shei Amsel (Raintree)

A Walk in the Desert. Caroline Arnold (Silver Press)

Videotape

Call or visit your local library to see if this videotape is available for your viewing.

The Desert. Barr Natural Science Series

Places to Write and Visit

Joshua Tree National
   Monument
74485 Monument Drive
Twenty-nine Palms, CA 92277

Death Valley
National Monument
Death Valley, CA 92328

Organ Pipe Cactus National
   Monument
Route 1, Box 100
Ajo, AZ 85321

Canadian Nature Federation
One Nicholas Street
Suite 520
Ottawa, Ontario K1N 7B7

Interesting Facts

1. Desert winds make dunes move and change shape. Dunes look like hills but, because they are made of sand, they can change shape.

2. The desert landscape changes so much each day that most people in the desert use the stars to guide them in their travels.

3. To keep from losing water through evaporation, some desert plants have very small leaves. Others have no leaves at all.

4. Many desert plants have sharp thorns or prickly stems to keep animals from eating them.

5. Birds and insects feed on the pollen and nectar of desert flowers.

6. With so little rain, desert plants need to scatter their seeds as widely as possible to catch any rain showers. The seeds of some desert grasses have spiky hooks that catch in the fur of passing animals. The animals carry the seeds off to various places.

7. Sometimes the desert wind uproots plants and blows them into new areas of the desert, where they may grow again.

8. Gazelles, antelope, and oryx have shiny coats that reflect heat from their bodies.

9. When a ground squirrel comes back to its burrow after being in the hot sun, it presses its belly against the walls to cool down.

10. The camel's long legs keep its body away from the hot desert floor.

Glossary

adapted: changed so that it is better able to survive.

burrows: small holes in the ground made by animals for shelter or living space.

camouflage: the coloring of the fur, feathers, or skin, or the shape of an animal that can make it difficult to see against its background.

herbivores: animals that eat plants in order to survive.

insulates: provides protection from the elements, such as the heat and cold.

oases: places in the desert where there is a source of water and plants can grow.

pollinate: to move a substance called pollen from a male part of a flower to a female part of the same or a different flower so that seeds may grow.

predator: any animal that kills another animal for food.

Index

32